Sweet Beatle Dreams

The Diary of Mary Mack Conger

Andrews and McMeel

A Universal Press Syndicate Company

Kansas City • New York

Conger, Mary Mack.
  Sweet Beatle dreams / Mary Mack Conger.
    p.   cm.
  ISBN: 0-8362-7975-1 : $6.95
    1. Conger, Mary Mack—Diaries.   2. Rock music fans—
United States—Diaries.   3. Beatles.   I. Title.
ML429.C58A3   1989
781.66′092—dc20   89-6964
[B]   CIP
                                                            MN

Designed by Rick Cusick

Attention: Schools and Businesses

Andrews and McMeel books are available at quantity
discounts with bulk purchase for educational, business,
or sales promotional use. For further information, please
write to: Special Sales Department, Andrews and McMeel,
4900 Main Street, Kansas City, Missouri 64112.

To my mother and father, who thought nothing good could ever come of all this.

Contents

"It was as if some savior had arrived and all these people were happy and relieved, as if things somehow were going to be better now."

Derek Taylor
Beatles' Press Officer, 1964

Preface

Nearly a quarter of a century has passed since a fourteen-year-old Iowa girl traveled to Chicago to see the Beatles perform during their first whirlwind tour across America in 1964. For me it was an impossible dream come true.

I wrote about that day and events preceding and following it in my diary. Little did I know then that I had chronicled in significant detail not only an important part of my own life, but also the start of a cultural earthquake.

I found that diary in my attic, and suddenly it was 1964. I was that teenaged girl again.

—Mary Mack Conger

Mary Mack at age fourteen—the Beatles have arrived in America!

CHAPTER 1

"All My Loving"

APRIL 10—

The Beatles are coming to the USA! It's true! Sue and I are making plans to see them at the Indiana State Fair. We're hoping Sue's sister can take us, but we'll get there if we have to crawl.

APRIL 11—

Mom says when I get older I will look back on these days and realize how silly I was. But how can I help it now?

The Beatles have the top two songs in the nation: No. 1, "Can't Buy Me Love," and No. 2, "Twist and Shout."

APRIL 12—

I broke the news to Sue today that Paul got married. Naturally, it broke her up. She said he should have waited for her. Let's just hope it's one big stupid rumor, and I really believe it is. If it is true, there's still George and Ringo, but I'd rather have John or Paul.

2

APRIL 13—

I'm finally out of my financial debt. I paid Mom the money I owed her and now I have $1.50 of my own. I have to start saving for Indianapolis.

Until tomorrow—

APRIL 14—

This town is a real hick town. I sure wish that I lived in England.

But here's some good news. Sue and I learned today that we don't have to go clear to Indianapolis to see the Beatles. They are going to be just next door in Chicago! Hey, maybe we could go both places. Now we have to work on Sue's sister to take us.

Where there's a will, there's a way. We have five whole months before the concert.

APRIL 15—

Chicago, here we come! Yep, Sue's sister said she'd take us there. Now I have to start pulling in the babysitting jobs.

More good news. Paul is not married. I repeat, he is NOT married. Sue and I bought a Beatle book tonight that said all of those marriage rumors are rubbish. Jolly good!

Got to go now. As always, I've left my homework until 11:00.

APRIL 16—

Brother, Saturday is going to be the coolest day. First of all, on "Bandstand" they're going to have a complete hour dedicated to the Beatles, with films and all. Also they're giving away hairbrushes . . . actually owned by the Beatles! I would die to have one.

Then, at 7:00, WLS is having a five-hour Beatle Spectacular, with a live, person-to-person call to all four of the Beatles. Is that cool?

Just watch me miss it. I have to babysit that night.

APRIL 17—

Made $3 babysitting last night. That's more towards my Beatles' fund.

Sue sent our ticket money in today. The tickets cost $3.50. I'm tired now. By-eeee-eeeee-eeee.

APRIL 18—

This was the perfect day for a Beatle Spectacular. "Can't Buy Me Love" is No. 1 in the nation again, but "Twist and Shout" dropped down to No. 3. Guess who took over the No. 2 spot? The Dave Clark Five! YUCK!

"Bandstand" was really good. They showed films of the Beatles arriving in the United States for "The Ed Sullivan Show" in February, and also their press conference.

The best part was on WLS. Ron Riley and Art Robbins had the Beatles on the phone for TWO HOURS! They talk so cool. At the time of the telephone call, it was 1:30 A.M. in

England. Paul, Ringo, John and George were at a recording session for their new movie called "A Hard Day's Night."

As Ron Riley says, "You have to think about that one for a while."

APRIL 19—

I just finished redecorating my room. It looks more "Beatle-ized" now.

I'm really in for it tomorrow! I didn't do any of my homework. All I did all day was listen to records and the radio. I also wrote a letter to Johnny Dean in London for a subscription to the "Beatles Monthly Magazine."

APRIL 20—

Mere routine today.

APRIL 26—

Favorite songs:
1. "Can't Buy Me Love"—The Beatles
2. "Love Me Do"—The Beatles
3. "Gonna Get Along Without You Now"—Skeeter Davis
4. "Romeo and Juliet"—The Reflections
5. "Do You Want to Know a Secret"—The Beatles
6. "Good Golly, Miss Molly"—Swingin' Blue Jeans
7. "It's Over"—Roy Orbison
8. "She's a Bad Motorcycle"—The Crestones

APRIL 27—

Sue isn't going to be the only one with "Love Me Do." I found out today that they are selling it down at Parkers Department Store. I still haven't used my record certificate that I won on KSTT, so I can get it free.

I really get tired of Sue always bragging about how much Beatle stuff she has. I remember when she had six Beatle magazines and I only had one. She sends away for everything as soon as she finds out about it.

APRIL 28—

Mom reminded me today about how I laughed and made fun of the Beatles the first time I saw their picture in "Life" magazine (or was it the "Post"?). They hadn't released their first record yet, and I had never even heard of them.

I can't believe that I laughed, but Mom says I did. I do remember that when they were on "The Ed Sullivan Show," I loved the way they sang, but that was it. I wasn't whipped or anything. Not like now.

I'm just so glad that I live during this Beatle-crazy time. Think of all the fun I'd be missing!

APRIL 29—

Oh no! We just heard the tickets are all sold out for Chicago, and we still haven't heard from Triangle Productions. Even if we do get a seat, it will probably be clear in the back. But that's okay with me.

Can you imagine? All the tickets sold out in only a few days!?

APRIL 30—

Friday night I went to the dance. I haven't been there for so long that I didn't even know any of the dances. In case when I get old my memory fails, I'd better list the dances we do so I can look back on them and remember what a nut I was.
(1) Monkey—this one is really wild, (2) Looey Looey,
(3) Slausen and (4) Beatle.

Right now I'm out trying to get a suntan. I'm as white as snow. Lake Canyada opens next month, so maybe I can get one there.

I got a couple of new Beatle books at Kresge's. There was a big article on (ugh!) THE Jane Asher in one of them. Brother, what a babe. I had a feeling that Paul would go for a different type—you know, the sweet and innocent type, like me.

I'm so confused. In that book it says that Paul probably IS married, but if he isn't, he is at least engaged. Oh, woe is me if he is engaged! He says he isn't, though, and that's good enough for me.

> *Signed,*
> *Mary McCartney*
> *(How's that for dreaming?)*

MAY 2—

Too busy to write today, so instead I'll fill this page with my favorite words. PAUL McCARTNEY, PAUL McCARTNEY, MARY AND PAUL, PAUL McCARTNEY.

7

MAY 4—

I finally got my Beatles Ltd. book today.

MAY 5—

Well, here we go again. This time they're marrying off Ringo, but I won't believe it. I have to have proof. Besides, on the front page of tonight's newspaper there was an article saying it isn't true. Ringo couldn't do that to me!

H.S.O.B.M.E.U.S.A. (Help Stamp Out Beatle Marriages in England and the USA.)

MAY 6—

Sue and I are thinking of peroxiding our hair this summer. Ringo, Paul and John are all taken, so that leaves George, and he likes blondes.

Oh, the Beatles have a new record out—it's "She Loves You"—in German! "Sie Lieb Diech," or something like that.

MAY 11—

WOW! WOW! WOW! DOUBLE WOW!!! KSTT just had a three-minute phone conversation with the Beatles, and it was cooler than heck! Here are some details:

Larry Cooper asked George if they had a barber, and George said, "No, that's just a dirty rumor." (I thought that was pretty cute.)

I ADORED the way Paul talked. He couldn't pronounce the word "exuberant." He said it real funny, but cute!

Oh, the most important part was, Larry asked Ringo if he was engaged, and then they all giggled. Rats, that's proof enough for me.

They said that their movie won't be released in the U.S. until the end of the year. That's so far away!

Well, I had better go—I've got to set my hair.

I'll write tomorrow. At least I'll TRY to.

MAY 16—

Sue stayed all night last night. She's in washing her hair now. Last night we decided we just couldn't wait any longer, so we called Triangle Productions. They said that tickets and refunds won't be sent out until June 15. That means we will have to wait until about the 20th to know. I won't be able to wait that long!

That call shot $1.25 to bits. That's how much it costs to call Chicago long distance.

MAY 17—

I entered three new Beatle contests today. For one contest, you had to write as many words as you can make from the letters in B-E-A-T-L-E-S. I found 77 in the dictionary. The prize is a stereo record player.

The other one is probably a big farce. You write in and put your phone number on a card, then the Beatles supposedly draw a card and call that person.

For the other one you write in 50 words why you would

like to go on a date with the Beatles. The prize is a date with a Beatle.

MAY 18—

Today Sue stayed all night with me and we slept outside— BRRRR! We froze. We were listening to WBZ and they read a letter from a girl in California who said that she heard a tape recording of George and Ringo saying that Paul is actually married to Jane Asher! I still won't believe it. No, no, no!

MAY 19—

Didn't do anything today.

MAY 21—

Thirteen more days of school!

MAY 22—

I've gotten quite a few new Beatle books since I last wrote. In one of them there was an offer for 12 Beatle pictures. I only had money for 6.

WOW—WOW—WOW! They're playing a song on WLS now that's written by Paul and John, but they don't sing in it. It's called "World Without Love." It is really sharp. BUT— guess who sings it? Give up? Jane Asher's brother!

MAY 23—

Well, tomorrow is the day I finally get my hair cut. I'm scared! I wanted long hair more than anything, but mine simply won't flip. I'm getting it cut into a blunt cut.

Today I requested "Love Me Do" on KSTT for all the Beatle fans.

MAY 25—

Today was neat. On "Ed Sullivan" they had an interview and a tape recording of THEM singing "You Can't Do That." They were all so cute, and they made a special point to be polite and nice to Ed. John even went out of his way to tell Ed that he would be looking forward to seeing him again. That just goes to show that adults are all wrong about them. They're actually very polite.

Next week the Dave Clark 5 is (are?) going to be on "Ed Sullivan."

Nine more days of school. YIPPEE!

MAY 26—

Oh brother, we ran the 600-yard dash in school today. I honestly thought I was going to die.

I don't really have anything else to say today, except, congratulations to me! I got an A on my Civics term paper!

Favorite records May 26:

1. "World Without Love"—Peter and Gordon
2. "Do You Love Me"—The Dave Clark 5
3. "I Understand Them"—The Pattycakes

4. *"Love Me Do"—The Beatles*
5. *"P.S. I Love You"—The Beatles*
6. *"Little Children"—Billy J. Kramer*

MAY 27—

Oh, this is complete misery! I stayed home from school today with an earache. I haven't eaten a thing all day. Maybe I can lose some weight!

We should be getting our "In His Own Write" books in the mail pretty soon. It's already on the bestseller list!

MAY 28—

Oh, this is terrible. I've never experienced such great pain in all my life. My head feels like I'm in a Russian torture chamber. I just sit and cry and cry until I'm afraid I've gone crackers.

Mom got me some medicine today, but it doesn't work.

MAY 29—

I forgot to tell you yesterday that I finally got that interview record in the mail from Apollo Distributors. Man, that's just like having THEM in the same room.

Hey, you know that Paul's mom died when Paul was only fourteen? Well, her name was Mary. Sue said that since his mom's name was Mary McCartney, we don't need another one. I say since his mom died, we really should have someone to take over her name. Don't you agree? Another Mary McCartney?

I went to the doctor today, and he gave me $11 worth of medicine. I think it's working.

P.S. Great news! "Suspicion" finally fell off the survey today. Gads, I'm sick of that song!

MAY 30—

Boy, I guess I have lost some weight! I tried on a dress today that hasn't fit me for a long time, but now it fits!

Today on WLS, Ron Riley called Louise Caldwell, George's sister, and asked her if those rumors about Ringo and Paul were true. She said they were "Ridiculous!" She said that if Paul and Ringo were ever to get married, their fans would be the first ones they'd tell. She also said that Paul feels very bad about people saying that he's conceited and affected.

Don't worry, Paul, I think you're wonderful!

MAY 31—

I take back everything bad that I ever said about the Dave Clark 5! I just saw them on "The Ed Sullivan Show," and I honestly think that they are neat! I'm not kidding you, I honestly think that Dave, Denny and Rick are sharp! Sue about killed me when I told her that I liked the DC5. She thinks I'm being disloyal to the Beatles.

I'm not going to school tomorrow, either. I think I'll use my day entering some more Beatle contests.

13

JUNE 1—

Well, today is June 1. This is the month when we will learn the truth. Will we get tickets, or won't we? We should find out about June 15.

I think I'm finally well. I'm going to school tomorrow, and then I only have three days left.

JUNE 2—

Well, today I went to school for the first time in 6 days. I haven't got too much work, forget that!

Sue and I are in hopes that her sister can take us to Chicago Saturday to see the Dave Clark 5 land. If we make a banner welcoming them, we could win passes to the show.

(Later.) Forget about going to see the Dave Clark 5. Sue just called me and said that her sister has to work Saturday.

Well, gotta go work on my speech, so I'll write tomorrow.

P.S. Here's a cute joke that I heard quite a while ago. I'm afraid I'll forget it, so I want to write it down: Once there were four Beatles, but now there are only three. Know why? Well, John got married and became a bedbug!

JUNE 3—

Color today blue. Ringo collapsed at a recording studio today. The doctor said it was not serious, he just had tonsilitis. But what if he died? That would be an international disaster! Please, Ringo, don't be sick for your USA tour!

I'm sitting here looking out the window at this bald guy mowing his lawn. He'd never make a Beatle, that's for sure!

JUNE 4—

Tomorrow is the last day of school. I never did get my make-up work done, so I can just imagine what my report card is going to be like.

The highlight of today is that Sue and I got our "In His Own Write" books. They are cooler than heck! I can hardly understand the stories or poems, although I "very much apprecialiate John Lenton's unintelligible effruings." Just looking at it is enough for me.

Well, gotta go.

JUNE 5—

School's out, school's out, teacher let the monkeys out!

Yep, today's the last day of school. I got my report card today. I got 4 As and 4 Bs. Not too bad, but next year I'm going to get in there and pitch and get straight As.

Boy, am I mad! Sue got her "Beatles Monthly" book from England today, and I haven't gotten mine yet. I even sent mine in before she did.

"Love Me Do" is No. 1 again this week on WLS and KSTT. Keep it up, boys!

JUNE 6—

Sue and I are trying to find a day that we can color our hair. It has to be a day that Mom works, so maybe we'll do it Tuesday.

Oh, no, what if our hair turns out pure blonde! I just want

mine lighter than it is now. Sue bought the box for the lightest color there is, and mine's the second lightest. I can't even imagine how it will turn out. Oh well, I'll be sure and let you know.

Mom gave me a $25 savings bond today for junior high graduation. That was nice of her!!

Favorite records June 6:

1. *"Can't You See That She's Mine"—Dave Clark 5*
2. *"Don't Let the Sun Catch You Crying"—Jerry and the Pacemakers*
3. *"My Guy"—Mary Wells*
4. *"Yesterday's Gone"—The Overlanders*
5. *"Don't Throw Your Love Away"—Millie Small*
6. *"Bad to Me"—Billy J. Kramer*

CHAPTER 2

"It Won't Be Long"

JUNE 7—

Today was the day! Sue got the reply from Triangle Productions. Were the tickets in the envelope? YES!!!! YES!!!!! Chicago, here we come! Our seats are in Row 48, seats 1 and 2. Now there's three whole months to wait.

"Love Me Do" is No. 1 again.

JUNE 9—

Man, I'm getting pretty fed up! I still haven't gotten my "Beatle Monthly." I bet something went haywire, 'cause I should have gotten it weeks ago.

The Searchers were on "The Tonight Show" last night. I just love their singing. A lot of people think they're queer, but I like them. They may not be the prettiest things on earth, but I just love the way they sing. Anyway, they come from Liverpool, so that makes them very good!!!

Oh, I colored my hair finally. It's a light brown with blonde highlights. It isn't light enough, so Sue and I are going to do it again.

18

JUNE 10—

I guess I'd better say something about Ringo. You might think he died or something. Well, he's getting better now. He'll be able to join the group by Friday so they can all go to Australia.

JUNE 11—

I'd say this is getting a little out of hand! I mean, I like the DC5 and all, but they're starting to butt in on the Beatles territory!

For about the past three months, the Beatles have had the top three requested songs on WLS, until last night when the DC5 had the second top requested song. It was "Can't You See That She's Mine." I think the reason is that last night they had a DC5 Spectacular that probably got everyone in a DC5-ish mood.

Ron Riley talked to Dave Clark on the phone (his accent isn't half as neat as the Beatles). He said they are supposed to come back to the U.S. in November, and that they are going to make a film. I'm sure it won't be nearly as good as the Beatles'.

JUNE 12—

The day isn't over yet, but there's nothing to do, so I thought I'd write in my diary. Today I made $2 toward my Beatle fund by helping Grandma clean her house. Sue and I were going to go to the show tonight, but she got canned, so I don't know if we can still go.

(Later.) Well, we did go to the show. I'm home now. We saw a sneak preview of "Bedtime Story," starring Marlon Brando and David Niven. It was about the funniest movie I've ever seen!

JUNE 13—

Well, Ringo's all better now. He joined John, Paul and George yesterday.

I wish the Beatles would hurry and get a new record! People are starting to say they are has-beens!

JUNE 15—

I spent the early afternoon sunbathing at my aunt and uncle's country club. Then Kathy called and wanted to know if I could help her lighten her hair. We walked to the shopping center and bought some peroxide, but she never did do it because Jeff came over, who, by the way, said all he could to run the Beatles down in front of me.

I'm getting sick and tired of everyone running down the Beatles.

IF YOU DON'T LOVE THE BEATLES, DON'T BUG ME!

JUNE 16—

Guess what! The Beatles are coming out with a new record next week. Two of them, in fact. Finally!

They are going to have an album of "A Hard Day's Night" with songs from their "flick." Also, they're releasing a new single called "Hard Day's Night." Sue said that Ron Riley said they will be released about the 29th of June.

All I can say is—it's about time!

JUNE 17—

Tomorrow is Paul's birthday. He'll be 22. We have to celebrate his birthday in some way, but how? Oh well, we'll think of something.

Mary Beth has been thinking that we would go to Chicago the Friday night before the Beatles' performance. We'd stay there Friday night and Saturday night. Pretty cool, eh? There goes at least $16. I have to start earning some more money fast!

JUNE 18—

Today was a big day—Paul's birthday.

In honor of Paul's birthday, WLS had a "Paul Spectacular." We missed out on part of it, because Sue and I were coloring our hair again. I learned two things about Paul that I didn't know before: His favorite color is blue, and his favorite song is "Hold Me Tight."

Boy, KSTT sure gave Paul a nice birthday present. "Love Me Do" dropped from No. 1 clear down to No. 5! Oh well, "A Hard Day's Night" will be in the No. 1 spot before long.

We tried to think of some way we could celebrate this red letter day, and we decided to bake Paul a cake. That's the least we could do! If only we lived in Chicago. They're having picnics and parties, and everything.

JUNE 19—

Because of our big night celebrating Paul's birthday last night, Sue and I did not get up until noon. All we did all day was write in our diaries—and something else. That something else was—call Liverpool!

I called the operator and told her that we would like to be connected with Information in Liverpool, England. We said we wanted the number of "John Waterhouse." I don't know where I got that name, it just sounded Liverpudlian to me.

The operator connected us with the overseas operator, who asked us if John Waterhouse is a member of a singing group. We said "no." Then she asked us what street he lives on. We didn't know, of course. She said she wouldn't put us through until we knew a little bit more about "John Waterhouse."

Then, out of sheer curiosity, we called the operator back to find out where the overseas operator is. She's in New York. JUST THINK . . . we actually talked to someone in New York!

We're going to go to the library sometime and try to find a phone directory of England so that we can get an authentic name and address in Liverpool. How's that for scheming? We're also going to look up the addresses and phone numbers of George, Ringo, John and Paul, and also Louise Caldwell.

Well, Mom just called and told me to get home, so I think I'd better go.

A faithful Beatlemaniac ———

Me

JUNE 20—

Well, Sue and I are at it again. She is mad at me because I told her that I can't go downtown today. I just don't have the money! Just because she gets as much money as she wants doesn't mean that I do. She's a spoiled brat! I just hope and pray that we're friends by September, or I'll be out of a ride to Chicago!

Last night Mom asked me if I changed the color of my hair. I said I had, and do you know what she said? She said she liked it! That's rather shocking, if you ask me!

JUNE 21—

In the morning "Times-Democrat" today, there was an article about John's book. But instead of putting John's picture in, they put George's in! Can you imagine someone making that mistake?

In the article, it said that the book has already sold 70,000 copies. That's pretty good, if you ask me. It is already No. 7 on the bestseller list.

Tonight at 9:00 on Channel 8, "Love Me Tender" is going to be on television. It stars the BIG E. This I've got to see! I think I've already seen it, as far as that goes.

JUNE 22—

I stayed all night at Chris Glass's house last night. We watched "Love Me Tender." It was so sad. I cried! I bawled! Of course, you realize that I'm not exactly the world's biggest Elvis fan, but I didn't want him to die!

Do you know what some people are doing? They bought up a whole bunch of tickets to the Beatles performance in Chicago. Now they're selling them for $50. That's plain scalpering!! I'm happy that we got ours when we did, but I imagine that if I had $50, I'd spend it on a Beatle ticket.

Peter and Gordon are coming to Chicago on July 10. Wish I could go. I love their new song.

JUNE 30—

I got my Beatle Fun Kit and my Paul McCartney pencils in the mail today. Called Sue right away and told her about all the mail I got. I'm writing this with my Paul McCartney pencil. Writes pretty good, huh?

"Hard Day's Night" has finally been released. But I don't know if you can buy it around here yet.

JULY 5—

This summer is going so fast. I don't have time to write in my diary anymore.

Today I found a little baby robin who had lost its mother. It had jumped in a can of oil, so it is very sick. I'm going to take care of it and see if I can make it well again. I named it Ringo, because of its beak.

JULY 6—

Today Karen and I walked over to Sue's house and looked at the pictures that she took on Paul's birthday. They're pretty good. I'm buying some reprints.

Tonight I went down to Karen's house. My hair was pinned up in toilet paper rolls. Karen said she wasn't having any company, but who should come along? STEVE! Embarrassing? Forget it!

JULY 7—

Went to see "Cleopatra" today. My bird died. It was Ringo's birthday.

Favorite records July 7:

1. "Nobody I Know"—Peter and Gordon

2. "Hard Day's Night"—The Beatles

3. "Don't Throw Your Love Away"—The Searchers

4. "I Get Around"—The Beach Boys

5. "Party Girl"—Bernadette Carol

6. "Rag Doll"—Four Seasons

7. "Wishin' and Hopin'"—Dusty Springfield

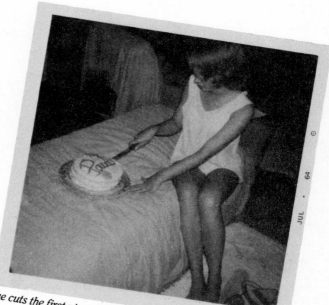

Sue cuts the first piece of Paul McCartney's birthday cake.

CHAPTER 3

"A Hard Day's Night"

JULY 8—

    I read an article in the paper today that said what a big hit the Beatles' movie is. It said that 20,000 people showed up for one showing, but they could only fit 2,000 in the theater. I can't wait! I can't wait!

JULY 10—

    John's book fell off the bestseller list. That's terrible.

JULY 11—

    Elvis won the Bandstand popularity contest. Sickening, much? Oh, well, have no fear, they're going to have a Beatles Spectacular July 25. It ought to be real good. On "Bandstand" today, they played "A Hard Day's Night" and "I Should Have Known Better." Then they took a poll to see which of the two was the more popular. "A Hard Day's Night" was.

JULY 12—

Sue made our Beatle trip reservations at a little motel in Chicago called *Lake Shore Drive Motel*. It will cost us about $15. My grand total that I have saved so far from babysitting and helping Grandma clean her house is $12. But I have to buy film and stuff, too.

JULY 13—

I learned today that the Rolling Stone's album beat out the Beatles album in England.

JULY 14—

Today I bought "A Hard Day's Night" and "I'll Cry Instead."

JULY 17—

I went to the Y-Dance last night. It was so hot that my hair went as straight as a board. I was so embarrassed, I could have cried.

JULY 18—

Karen and I made a pizza today. What a mess. It was uneatable, so we made another one.

I babysat tonight and made some Chicago money. But I spent some yesterday. So now, my grand total is $12.18.

JULY 20—

Steve called. I like him so much.

Today on WLS they played the brand new Beatles album. Guess what it's called? "Something New."

JULY 25—

Questions asked by Dick Clark on "Bandstand's" Beatle Spectacular:

Q. How many of you have bought Beatle material in the last three weeks?

A. Almost all of them.

Q. How many of you think the Beatles will be as popular by Christmas?

A. Almost all of them.

Q. How many of you are tired right now of the Beatles?

A. Almost all of them.

AUGUST 1—

It's been a long time since I've written about the Beatles. It's not because I don't like them; I just don't have time to think about them. I still love them! But sometimes I think I like Steve just a teensy-weensy bit better. Is that okay?

"A Hard Day's Night" is coming August 12.

Dick Clark's Caravan of Stars is coming September 1. Guess who is going to be host?!?!?—FABIAN!

AUGUST 3—

Steve Wilkerson, Steve Wilkerson, Steve Wilkerson. (Mack, you're a swine!)

AUGUST 4—

The heat is on in Vietnam again. There is another war threat. Oh well.

AUGUST 9—

There is going to be a war soon. World War III may come any minute now. For some reason I am not so scared as I was last summer when there was a war threat. I try very hard not to think too far into the future. I just take life as it comes.

AUGUST 10—

Favorite records:
1. "A Hard Day's Night"—The Beatles
2. "I Should Have Known Better"—The Beatles
3. "House of the Rising Sun"—The Animals
4. "Things We Said Today"—The Beatles
5. "How Do You Do It"—Gerry and the Pacemakers
6. "And I Love Her"—The Beatles
7. "I Like Bread and Butter"—The New Beats
8. "It Hurts to Be in Love"—Gene Pitney

AUGUST 12—

Oh, brother, I don't like anyone today. Guess what? I found out last night that Steve really likes Karen and not me. I hate him! He says he wants me to forget about him, but I can't! I won't! I never will!!

Why are boys so mean?

AUGUST 13—

I got a letter from Greg Ludtke today. He's so nice. I also saw John Michaelson— at the A&W Root Beer stand. He said I'd be seeing him around. I sure hope so!

Boy! I sure wish I had a lock and key for this diary! What if someone finds it and gets curious?

AUGUST 14—

I looked up the Beatles' names in a name derivation book from the grocery store today. Here's what they mean: John means "God's gracious gift," George means "farmer," Richard (for Ringo) means "stern king," and Paul means "small."

I'm going to Younkers tomorrow to see if I can find a dress to wear to Chicago. I want it to be something special. I've already bought some Beatle boots.

AUGUST 15—

"A Hard Day's Night" is finally here! It starts tomorrow. All the tickets are already sold out for the first day. I hope I can go Monday night.

AUGUST 17—

A red letter day! Brother, "A Hard Day's Night" isn't too neat or nothing, forget that! I have never seen such an exciting movie.

Karen, Chris and I sat through it twice at the RKO Orpheum Theater. We went at 5:00 and stayed until 10:30. I wanted to sit through it again, but Mom and Dad wouldn't pick us up that late.

I mean it, the moment the movie went on the screen, everyone in the whole place screamed, except me. I cried, I sobbed! Somehow the music has that effect on me. I can't help it.

The best scene was when the Beatles were goofing around on a soccer field. Oh, how I wish I could see the movie again.

While we were waiting for my parents to pick us up, we met some girls who are also going to Chicago to see the Beatles. Guess where their seats are! The tenth row! Those scums.

Off to see the Beatles! From left to right, Mary Beth, Sue and Mary

Lines formed early for the concert—we spotted a Beatle look-alike.

CHAPTER 4

"Twist and Shout"

AUGUST 18—

Welcome to the U.S.A., Beatles! They arrived at Los Angeles today at 7:47 and then flew to San Francisco.

Here is their itinerary: August 19, San Francisco; 20th, Las Vegas; 21st, Seattle; 22nd, Vancouver; 23rd, Hollywood; 26th, Denver; 27th, Cincinnati; 28th, New York; 30th, Atlantic City.

September 2nd, Philadelphia; 3rd, Indianapolis; 4th, Milwaukee; 5th, Chicago; 6th, Detroit; 7th, Toronto; 8th, Montreal; 11th, Jacksonville; 12th, Boston; 13th, Baltimore; 14th, Pittsburgh; 15th, Cleveland; 16th, New Orleans; 18th, Dallas; 20th, New York.

AUGUST 20—

Karen and I went to the fair tonight and saw Brenda Lee perform. She was good! We played some games on the midway, and we really got gypped. Between us, we lost something like $3. There goes my Chicago money.

That's about all I have to say, except, I LOVE THE BEATLES!

AUGUST 23—

The Beatles were on "Ed Sullivan" today. Oh, it was so cool. George is just too neat for words. Of course, so are the other three, but George is a little more special!!! W.O.W.

School starts in less than a week. But more important is that it is only 11 days until we go to Chicago. I can't believe it. I just can't believe it. I know it's true, but I just can't believe it. I'm finally going to get to see the Beatles in person.

I wrote two letters to two girls in England today. I got their names from "Beatles Monthly" (yes, I finally got it). I hope one of them becomes my pen pal. I sure want to know a lot about England.

AUGUST 29—

I still can't believe it. Just think, in less than a week, we will be in Chicago. And one week from tonight, we'll actually be seeing the Beatles in person! Gloryosky!!

I babysat tonight and made $3.50. I now have $17.10. That isn't very much, considering I have to buy movie film and regular film. I hope my brother lets me use his camera. I must remember to take his binoculars, too.

"And I Love Her" is No. 1 on "Bandstand." "I'll Cry Instead" is No. 6.

AUGUST 31—

I spent practically all day downtown today. I got some Beatle pins and some more blonde junk. I hope it works.

SEPTEMBER 1—

Today was high school orientation day. Boy, is West big! I think I'm actually going to like it.

Sue dyed her hair again. She called me up tonight and told me in despair that it is black! This I've got to see!!!!

SEPTEMBER 3—

One day until blastoff.

This day I will never forget. I don't have time to explain it all, but to get down to facts, this is the day Karen and I had orange hair. That's right. ORANGE HAIR!! Orange. I thought I was going to have to go to Chicago like that. Thank God the lady gave us some stuff to fix it.

SEPTEMBER 4—

The day is here at last. I worried the whole trip that I left my ticket at home. I made several trips back to the trunk of the car to be sure that it was there. Sue and I took sack lunches along to eat on the way so that we could save some money. But I hadn't planned on spending so much money on the tollways.

Our motel is really a slick place. It has elevators, air-conditioning in every room, television and a swimming pool.

We have already met the lifeguard. He's 19 and a real doll. Sue told him that we were 18. He told us about a beach party set for Monday night (a real orgy, probably, he said). Too bad we can't go.

The first thing we did after unpacking was hit the

to spend hours getting ready fo
took 15 minutes! That's a recor
look the best it could, and my r
we hurriedly grabbed our cam
and rushed back to the theater.

By that time there were lots
nice chats with a few policeme
to-eye on my favorite subject—

There were a lot of nice peo
dressed differently. Some girls
like Sue and me. Others had c
ragged gym shoes. There wer
leather or suede, Beatle hats,
Sue and I stayed and talke
that they were carrying Beatl
Later a man came along selli
match our outfits. I got red; S

At about 4:00, Sue and I u
ordered Beatle Burgers and p
juke box. I was so excited I sp
place. I saved my check, bec
wrote. She wrote "Biddle Bu
the Beatles were! Spare me!

We were sitting there talk
talk to us. He said that the B
London, and they wouldn't l
knew this wasn't true, howe
the United States, not Londo

When we got back we dis
line, so we had to go to the
There was a whole crew

this night, but instead, we
for us both. My hair didn't
ylons had runs in them. But
ras, binoculars and purses,

more people there. I had some
, but we sure didn't see eye-
the Beatles.
le there, and everyone was
had regular dress-up clothes,
t-offs, Beatle buttons and
girls who had on a lot of
dark eyes and black socks.
to girls in the line. We noticed
pennants, and we wanted one.
g them, so we bought one to
we got green.
nt across the street to eat. We
ayed Beatle records on the
illed my orange pop all over the
use it is so funny what the lady
er!" She didn't even know who

g when some man started to
atles' plane had broken down in
able to make it to Chicago. We
er, because the Beatles were in
. Give us a break!
covered we had lost our place in
nd.
of adults trying to maintain some

order outside the theater. Blockades were set up all around. Only people with tickets were allowed on that side of the street.

Every once in a while the crowd would start screaming. Someone would think she saw a Beatle, and then everyone would get hysterical. Once when everyone was screaming, I moved out of line to see what all the excitement was. Unfortunately, I stepped over the line we had been warned about. Therefore, it was back to the end of the line for me.

At about 5:00 P.M., two rescue trucks came. But there were still three-and-a-half hours until the performance! What did they think was going to happen?

Finally, about an hour later, the doors were opened. Sue and I had our first look at the Amphitheater. It was certainly nothing fancy, but it was gigantic.

We bought a really cool Beatle book in the lobby and then went to find our seats. We kept walking closer . . . and closer . . . and closer to the front. Row 52 . . . 51 . . . 50 . . . 49 . . . 48. Row 48, Seat 2. We couldn't believe how close our seats were to the stage!

The time before the show passed quickly. We talked to strangers and even got a few addresses for pen pals. We took pictures of Ringo's drums. Those pictures will always be among my most prized possessions, I am sure.

When THEY finally started singing (after Jackie DeShannon and the Righteous Brothers), you couldn't even hear them. Not at all. It was one solid scream. John told the crowd to clap their hands instead of screaming. Of course, that didn't work. It just made us scream louder.

My favorite song they sang was "Things We Said Today." George sings most of it, but Paul sings, too.

I love you, Beatles, I always will!

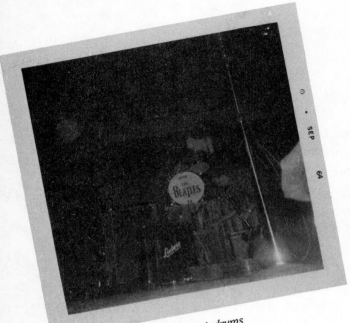

The stage crew setting up Ringo's drums

The official program and ticket stub

CHAPTER 5

"I'll Cry Instead"

SEPTEMBER 7—

Well, it's over and I could just cry. This is something I will never forget for the rest of my life. Sue and I wrote the Beatles' signatures on our arms, and we're telling everyone that the Beatles wrote them. Everyone believes us. I don't know when we will tell them the truth.

SEPTEMBER 12—

Wonderful news! Next October 10, "Bandstand" is having another Beatle Spectacular. That's a little bit of all right!

Favorite records September 12:

1. "Pretty Woman"—Roy Orbison
2. "Last Kiss"—J. Frank Wilson
3. "Do Wa Di Di Di"—Manfred Mann
4. "It's All Over Now"—The Rolling Stones
5. "Someday We're Going to Love Again"—The Searchers
6. "Dancin' in the Street"—Martha and the Vandellas
7. "We'll Sing in the Sunshine"—Gale Garnett
8. "Come a Little Bit Closer"—Jay and the Americans

SEPTEMBER 13—

John's birthday is on October 9th and the Beatle Spectacular is on the 10th. I want Sue to stay all night with me on John's birthday, so we can celebrate!

I bought two of the neatest Beatle books today.

SEPTEMBER 14—

Well, here we go again. We might get to see the Beatles again! That's right! A friend of mine heard on the radio last night that the Beatles will be coming back to America sometime soon. I knew it in my bones. I knew I'd see them again.

SEPTEMBER 16—

I'm so proud of my English test. Not only did I get a "96 Excellent," but Miss Boland wrote "Please come to class on test days. This kind of test is the teacher's thanks for aching feet and tired tonsils!" I want to be an English teacher just like her someday.

OCTOBER 6—

Hi Stranger!

I haven't had time to write because I am so busy with school. What's new? I am madly in love with Ed Lemon. He is the neatest sophomore at West. But more about him later. Right now I have to say something about my very favorite subject—the Beatles.

Yeah, I'm still in love with those four fab mopheads. In fact, I'm so wrapped up in them it hurts. I mean, it really hurts inside.

I am so depressed that our Chicago trip is over. Maybe if I took down all my Beatle pictures, put away everything pertaining to them and never talked about them, then maybe I could forget about it.

They have a new record out called "I'll Be Back." I haven't heard it yet, but it is always being mentioned on WBZ.

The Beatles are going to be on "Shindig" tomorrow night. I won't miss that for the world!!!

Well, I'm going to quit writing about the Beatles now, because it makes me sad.

To make it worse, Sue and I aren't best friends anymore. Something happened. She never calls me anymore. We don't even talk to each other in the halls anymore. This really makes me feel bad. This Friday we were supposed to celebrate John's birthday at my house, but I gather that's all called off.

Well, let's talk about something more pleasant, like Ed. What a doll! Everyone keeps telling me that he likes me. But he could have the pick of any girl he wanted.

OCTOBER 9—

Happy Birthday, Johnny my Luv! And may you have many more happy ones!

Sue stayed all night with me tonight, after all. We got home at midnight and then made John a cake. The cake wasn't as good as Paul's, but that's okay. It was chocolate with white frosting, and it had "John" written in green frosting.

To top the night off, we were listening to the radio—and guess what we heard!!! "I'll Be Back." It was on WBZ, so the reception wasn't very good, but what we did hear was gear! I hope they will start playing it around here pretty soon.

OCTOBER 10—

Favorite records:
1. *"I'll Be Back"—The Beatles*
2. *"You Really Got Me"—The Kinks*
3. *"Have I the Right?"—The Honeycombs*
4. *"She's Not There"—The Zombies*

OCTOBER 11—

Today in the paper there was an article about these two girls from Cleveland who ran away to England to see the Beatles. They withdrew $2,000 from their parents' bank account and then took off. I'd love to hear the details. Sue and I wanted to be the first ones to run away to England, but I guess they beat us to the punch. They were actually in London for 21 days!

Someday I'm going to go to England. I've wanted to go ever since I was in fourth grade and studied about the Queen and castles. Now, because of the Beatles, I want to go even more.

Sue is starting to put aside $5 each week to go to England someday.

Modeling the latest fashion in front of some favorite Beatle posters

CHAPTER 6

"Hold Me Tight"

OCTOBER 19—

The world is in a horrible mess. On October 15 Khrushchev resigned. I don't know whether he resigned or whether he was kicked out, but I think it was the latter. I've always wondered what would happen if Khrushchev died, or whatever. I guess now we'll find out.

Also, Red China has the nuclear bomb now. So that's another worry. Oh well. Why worry? I mean, if we're going to get blown up, I don't guess there's anything I can do about it.

OCTOBER 20—

I just happened to think of something. My diary can become another "Diary of Anne Frank." I mean, if there is a war, or when we are all dead and gone, someone might dig up my diary someday and publish it. Oh, Lordy! To whomever is reading this diary years from now: Don't think that everyone was this crazy in '64!

50

OCTOBER 22—
   Go West. Beat Central.

OCTOBER 23—
   Karen and I dressed up really "mod" to go to the football game last night. My parents said we looked like spooks. They dropped us off a block away from the stadium so that no one would see us with them. A lot of people didn't like our boots.

OCTOBER 24—
   We went to see Jane Asher (ASS-er) in "Masque of the Red Death" today. Her face looks like an angel, but she sure is skinny, and she has freckles all over her body. I have to admit it, though, we're jealous. She's a very lucky girl.
   Oh, well, she can have Paul. I'll take George.

OCTOBER 25—
   Up with the Rolling Stones! They were on "The Ed Sullivan Show" tonight, and I think they are gear! I don't care much for Charlie or Bill, but the other three are great, especially Brian and Keith. I forget which one is which, but the blond one has beautiful hair. It's really smooth and shiny. The other one, the one who stands on the right side of Mick, reminds me so much of George. WOW!
   The Stones aren't as well-groomed or gentlemanly as the Beatles, but there's something about them I like. After they

51

sang, Mick came over and shook Ed Sullivan's hand and thanked him.

The Stones don't dress alike while on stage. Mick dresses sort of sloppily. In fact, I think he had a sweatshirt on. Gads!

The teenagers went wild when they were singing. They screamed and screamed, even after the Stones left the stage. Nothing Ed Sullivan could do or say could stop the screaming.

"The Ed Sullivan Show" is really a good show. They always have someone real neat as guests. Next week the Dave Clark 5 will be on again. Sometimes I like them, but then sometimes they bug me.

Billy J. Kramer is going to be on "Shindig" this week.

OCTOBER 26—

EEE-GADS! I had a dream last night to top all dreams! It was a perfect set up, but something fouled up somewhere. It went something like this:

The Beatles were going to come to Iowa State, and they were going to stay with my brother. Anyway, they were going to spend a quiet night in the house, and Tom said I could come over if I wanted to.

Oh, my God, this was a chance in a lifetime, I thought. At last I was going to get to know George.

When I was ready, I went to Tom's house. I rang the doorbell, and I heard four Liverpudlian voices call out, "Come in, Luv." I opened the door and walked in.

Now this is the crazy part. I went inside, and who did I see?

52

Sprawled all over the living room furniture, relaxing and enjoying themselves, were the Beatles . . . yes, they were the Beatles . . . but they were NEGROES!

Now figure that one out, if you can.

OCTOBER 27—

Today was a slightly depressing day. I cleaned up my room and went through my Chicago souvenirs. I think I must have saved a piece of everything I touched in Chicago. I still even have my ticket stub. I wrapped it up in toilet paper and put it in a little metal box stuffed with cotton. Then I wrapped about a million rubber bands around it. It should be safe now. I want to keep it forever.

I just can't believe I have seen the Beatles. I just can't believe it.

OCTOBER 28—

Today was Career Day at school. A bunch of stuffed shirts came and talked to us about careers. Bore. Bore. Bore.

It was also "Dress-up Day" so we could give our visitors a good impression. I wore my orange angora sweater and dyed-to-match skirt.

OCTOBER 30—

I was going to go to the Y dance tonight, but I didn't have any money. Karen says I didn't miss out on much. But she said one of the boys in the combo looked just like Paul.

What does she mean, I didn't miss out on much?

NOVEMBER 4—

Gerry and the Pacemakers were on "Shindig" tonight. Gerry monkeyed at the end.

NOVEMBER 8—

Favorite records:
1. *"Any Way You Want It"—Dave Clark 5 (no fooling!)*
2. *"Time Is on My Side"—Rolling Stones*
3. *"You Really Got Me"—The Kinks*
4. *"Baby Love"—The Supremes*
5. *"She's Not There"—The Zombies*
6. *"I Like It"—Gerry and the Pacemakers*
7. *"Mountain of Love"—Johnny Rivers*

NOVEMBER 9—

I went to the store to buy a stamp for a letter to my pen pal. I wrote "Ringo for President" all around the stamp before I handed the letter back for the lady to mail for me. She told me that what I had done was illegal.

Oh, really? She should have seen some of my other envelopes!

NOVEMBER 10—

Wow! We are in for a treat! "The Entertainers" with Carol Burnett is going to be about the Beatles Friday night, and there's going to be another hour-long show about them on Sunday called "Around the Beatles." Coolness!

NOVEMBER 11—

The Rolling Stones were on the "Red Skelton Show" last night. Jane Willard saw them in person and said their hair is horrid. But I really like them. Besides, they sang a song about me! Mary Mack!

NOVEMBER 13—

Friday the 13th!

Everything has gone great today. I heard it! I really did! I heard "I Feel Fine" on the radio tonight. Oh, it is marvy! I know it wasn't supposed to come out until November 27, but KDKA must have it ahead of time.

After that, "The Beatles in America" with Carol Burnett was on. Murray the K was the official host.

NOVEMBER 14—

I wrote to my pen pal in England today. I hope to heaven she writes me back.

I can't wait to see Mike Chapin in school tomorrow. What a doll.

It is now 8:00 P.M. American time; 2:00 A.M. London time.

On WLS, Ron Riley is telling the top six songs from the
British Billboard. Here they are:
  1. "Always Something There to Remind Me"—Sandy Shaw
  2. "Pretty Woman"—Roy Orbison
  3. "Baby Love"—Supremes
  4. "Sha-La-La"—Manfred Mann
  5. "Walk Away"—Mat Monroe
  6. "The Wedding"—Julie Rogers

NOVEMBER 15—

"Round the Beatles" was on tonight. They sang 7 or 8 of
their top songs and did a parody of a scene from
Shakespeare's play, "A Midsummer Night's Dream." Other
guests were Millie Small, Celia Black, P.J. Proby, Long John
Baldry, the Vernon Girls and the Jets.

The best part was when P.J. Proby sang "Walking the
Dog," which starts out "Mary Mack, dressed in black!"
That's me! Mary Mack! And then right after him, a girl sang a
song saying how she'd like to know Mary Mack. Why do they
all sing about Mary Mack, I wonder? There have been other
songs with my name in it, too. Mom said it must be easy to
find words to rhyme with that name.

I think I read "Midsummer Night's Dream" once, but I
didn't really recognize this parody of it. At the end of the
show, John said, "Thank you very much. God bless you. You
know you've got a lucky face. The end."

NOVEMBER 20—

Sue got a letter from her pen pal today. She sounds like a pretty good one, although not as good as mine. I just hope to God that mine writes back. Just to make sure I'm kept up on things in England, I think I'll write to some more girls and see if they write back.

I went to the Y dance last night and met the coolest guy. He's a surfer from California! Gads, what a doll! You should have seen the way he did the jerk.

I can't wait until I go to California. Oh, didn't you know I was going to California? I'm planning on going to college out there. I think Mom is behind me on this.

Well, let's get back to talking about the surfer. He had on a blue sweatshirt and tan jeans. We were standing by the combo talking when a policeman came up and told him that he had to leave because he was wearing a sweatshirt.

Now I'll never see him again.

Favorite songs November 20:
"Ringo"—Lorne Green
"She's a Woman"—Beatles
"I Feel Fine"—Beatles

NOVEMBER 22—

Gads, this day brings back memories.

I'll never forget this day last year. All of a sudden the radio started playing on the intercom at school. I figured a secretary had pushed a wrong button. But then we heard that Kennedy had been shot, and then we heard he was dead. School was dismissed, and nobody said a word in the halls

*or on the way home. It was real dark and gray outside. We
went straight home and turned on TV and didn't leave the TV
for four days.*

*The worst part I remember was when John-John saluted
his dad's casket.*

*Pretty soon I'm going to have to buy a new diary. There
goes $2, but just think of everything I have to look back on.*

NOVEMBER 28—

*Keith Miller told me tonight after school that Ray Burner
likes me. He's nice, but I don't like him for a boyfriend. Here's
the list, in order, of guys I like right now.*

1. Tom Felix

2. Mike Chapin

3. Ed Lemon

*Oh, I forgot! Paul, George, John and Ringo. They go at the
very top, of course.*

DECEMBER 1—

*Beatle news! Ringo is to have his tonsils out at 8:00 A.M.,
December 2, London time; 3:00 A.M., Boston time and 2:00
A.M., our time. He is at University College Hospital, London.
WLS is going to call Ringo this week. Anyone who wants to
(or can afford to) can call the hospital for a three-minute
report of his condition. The number is Covent Garden 2332.
But to call London from Chicago, it costs $12.*

*"Beatles for Sale," the Beatles new album, is going to be
released the day after tomorrow in England. The USA*

version is "Beatles '65." It will be out the end of December or beginning of January.

DECEMBER 2—

Well, as of 2:00 this morning, Ringo is without his tonsils. I wonder how he sounds. I sure hope he doesn't sound like Karen did when she had her tonsils out. That was awful.

Today the student council from Central came to observe our school. There were some pretty cool boys. Ricky Rathman came. He still likes me. No one can figure out why I don't like him.

DECEMBER 3—

Here's an update on Ringo: Last night he watched the telly in his red pajamas. WBZ called the hospital at 1:00 A.M. London time. The hospital report said he's been eating ice cream, tea and specially cooked eggs. He should be sitting up by Friday.

DECEMBER 4—

Nothing prodigious (one of my new vocabulary words) happened today. I couldn't go to the dance because I had to babysit.

Oh, I do wish my pen pals would write back! I think I'll write Sally once more. I hope she doesn't think I'm a leech.

DECEMBER 5—

Mrs. Holdridge gave me her "Cosmopolitan" magazine with an article about John Lennon. The picture of him on the cover was the neatest!

I learned today how to write "Beatles," "Paul," "George," and "Ringo" using the Greek alphabet. In Greek letters, "Ringo" looks like "Pluto." I can't figure out how to write "John" because I think the Greeks didn't use any "J's."

DECEMBER 6—

To my everloving diary:

I didn't do anything today except study and give Donnie Cooper the brush-off. I hope he finally took the hint. He's been calling me every night. ICK!

I'll stick to my Beatles, thank you.

DECEMBER 7—

Hi!

DECEMBER 10—

I wonder if a Beatle song is No. 1 on KSTT tonight? I'll soon know.

Yes! "I Feel Fine" is No. 1. It made No. 1 in just 14 days.

Tonight I met a lady who used to live 40 miles from Liverpool. That lucky stiff! She had the coolest accent!

By the way, Chris Glass has really mastered the Liverpool

accent. Now, whenever she meets someone new, she tricks them into believing she's from England.

DECEMBER 11—

I had a riot tonight. First of all, I went to the game. The game wasn't too much fun, but then I went to the dance, and that was a lot of fun. I danced with this real neat kid with a Beatle haircut. His name is Reggie, and he plays the guitar. My parents would never let him in our front door, though, so I don't dare ever invite him over.

I think Sue likes Ed Lemon now. She can have him, because I like Kenny Cagney. Kathy Davis and Pam Marron like him, too. Of course, I still like Tom, too.

DECEMBER 12—

I babysat tonight and made $3. While I was babysitting, I heard on WLS that the Beatles will be coming to America the last part of March or the early part of April. Oh, it'd be so cool if I got to see them on my birthday. What a birthday present!!!!

"I'm a Loser" was third most requested song on WLS and "Everybody Wants to Be My Baby" (sung by George) was second. That's the way to hang in there, boys!

DECEMBER 13—

Oh gads, I can't wait until December 20. Why? Because "A Hard Day's Night" is coming back to the RKO Orpheum! Sue and I are going to go see it every day. I wish I could take my camera and take pictures. Would they turn out, I wonder?

I can't wait until tomorrow to see Kenny.

DECEMBER 14—

Hi, creep! How are things?

I just can't wait until Sunday when I see that movie again! I know I'm going to cry through the whole thing!

I really do like Kenny, but he is shorter than me. I hope he goes to the Y dance Friday.

Happy Birthday, Dave Clark! Yeah, tomorrow is his birthday. He'll be 22. Hip, hip and all that!

DECEMBER 15—

The Dovells were just on the "Lloyd Thaxton Show." I really like them, but it seems that all the groups are trying to copy the way the Beatles joke around on stage. Maybe it is just my imagination.

DECEMBER 16—

Today I ironed my hair. No lie! I'm going to wear it this way to the Beatle movie on Sunday. I love it!

The Dave Clark 5 were on "Shindig." WOW! I think Dave and Mike are dolls. Gads, their pants were skin-tight.

DECEMBER 17—
  "Beatles '65" is now for sale. I can't wait to get it.

DECEMBER 18—
  Oh, I really like Kenny! Randy Barrett likes me, according to Tom Green. But I just like him as a friend. Today I walked down the hall with Kenny. Jeanne and Kathy saw me walking with him. Jeanne wants Kenny to like Pam Marron, and Kathy wants him to like her, but I want him to like me!!!! I wonder who he likes?!?!?
  I sure hope he goes to the game.

DECEMBER 19—
  Central clobbered us last night in the biggest game of the year.

DECEMBER 20—
  Saw "A Hard Day's Night" again. No time to write. Busy, busy.

DECEMBER 21—
  IF YOU LOVE THE BEATLES, SMILE . . . IF YOU DON'T, DON'T BOTHER TO SMILE. THIS IS NO LAUGHING MATTER.

63

DECEMBER 22—

"Et tu, Brute!" I got an A on my Julius Caesar composition! Hooray!

DECEMBER 29—

It's almost the end of the year.
I wonder what 1965 will bring. Another Beatles concert? A war? Another president assassinated?

DECEMBER 30—

Well, there are only 26 hours left of 1964. Then I will put this year's diary away in a secret hiding place. This has truly been the year of the Beatles.

Things will change—we will all grow up and old. Even the Beatles. What will the future hold?

I intend to continue to write about my experiences in a diary for 1965. Will that be another "Year of the Beatles?" I hope so!

Yours sincerely,
Mary Mack, 1964

1964—That was a good year (I guess).

CHAPTER 7

"Beatles '65"

JANUARY 1—

Happy New Year!

Last night was New Year's Eve, and I didn't do anything but babysit. Whee! Everyone else was out having a good time, and I was babysitting.

I'm SO glad I'm going to have a diary this year.

Guess what I got for Christmas? A guitar! I'm so happy! But I already broke a string trying to tune it. Stupid me.

I went to Sue's house today and we made up a long list of all the things we have in common with the Beatles. George and I have the same boot size, Paul and I are both left-handed, but John and I are the most alike. We do what we want and what people think of us doesn't matter. And we both like to write. Also, we seem to have the same outlook on everything, such as parents, adults, politics, etc. That's good, because John is my favorite Beatle now.

JANUARY 2—

Last night Sue and I went to the "Good Guy Go-Go." We LOVE the Night People. We dance in the front and stare at them all night. I know they know we are staring.

JANUARY 3—

Sue and I got up the nerve to call Rob Dahms of the Night People today. We called all the Dahms in the phone book and finally found the right one. But the moment Rob said hello, Sue hung up.

She finally convinced me to call him back, so I did. We said our names were Cindy and Karen. He was real nice and we talked for quite a while. He said he would dedicate a song to us Sunday at the "Go-Go."

JANUARY 5—

Mom is starting to get after me about my room. I don't really blame her. There isn't much room for anything else, when the closet is stacked sky-high with Beatle magazines. But I just love reading and saving everything about the Beatles. During these last two months there have been 29 articles (I counted them!) in the "Times-Democrat." What am I going to do when people stop writing about them?

"I Feel Fine" and "She's a Woman" are No. 1 in the states now. Way to hang in there, boys! Their new album, "Beatles '65" has just been released, and if it isn't cool! I just LOVE "Rock and Roll Music"! I'd give anything to have the British

album "Beatles for Sale," because they sing "Kansas City" on it, the song they sang on "Shindig."

Favorite songs January 5:

1. "I Feel Fine"—The Beatles
2. "Anyway You Want It"—The Dave Clark 5
3. "I'm into Something Good"—Herman's Hermits
4. "Mountain of Love"—Johnny Rivers
5. "You've Lost that Lovin' Feeling"—The Righteous Brothers

JANUARY 6—

I finally got a letter from Sally today. She filled me in on everything in jolly old Leicester, England.

Sally says she's bats about the "Pretty Things" and "The Animals." There are so many groups to be wild about in England. But me, I remain loyal through and through to the Beatles.

I love the way she writes. She says she has been ill in bed "for a fortnight now." She calls boys "chaps" and uses different expressions. I wish that I lived in England!

She is neither a Mod nor a Rocker. "Call me a Mocker," she writes. Rockers are mainly teenagers who wear leather clothes and ride motor bikes. Mods wear fashionable clothes, etc.

JANUARY 7—

A lot of my girlfriends have been piercing each others' ears lately. That's the style. Maybe I'll get up enough nerve to do it someday. First you freeze your ear with an ice cube. Then, when it's bright red, you stick a needle through your earlobe into a potato.

They say it doesn't hurt. It just stings for a little while.

FEBRUARY 2—

Right now I'm in my room listening to my Barry McGuire album. I LOVE it! I wish I could play those songs on my guitar. I love the way he sings "You don't believe . . . we're on the eve of de-struct-ion!"

Gary Berger just called me. What a riot he is!

FEBRUARY 5—

I started my first real job today! No more babysitting for me. I work at Mercy Hospital in the cafeteria. I like my job, and there are a lot of cute boys there.

FEBRUARY 10—

I got another letter from Sally today. I had asked her if it is true that English boys wear mascara and eye shadow. She said yes! Can you believe it? She said that a group of mod boys in London started the craze. They also wear hair lacquer (hair spray), perfume, face powder and eyeliner.

That's bloody stupid. I wouldn't go near any boy who looked like that.

FEBRUARY 11—

Ringo got married to Maureen yesterday. Brother, she's only 18 years old. I heard her on a radio interview, and I don't think she sounded very intelligent. I bet it doesn't last.

Favorite songs February 11:
"Downtown"—Petula Clark
"Love Potion #9"—The Searchers
"She's a Woman"—The Beatles
"The Name Game"—Shirley Ellis

MARCH 15—

Mom is really upset with me today. She says that the Beatles have ruined my whole personality. She says if I don't snap out of it pretty soon, I am never going to amount to anything.

APRIL 2—

It's 9:00 P.M. I just got home from my job at the hospital. Since I started to work, I don't have time to write in my diary anymore.

Tonight at work I served at a banquet for the priests. Sister Laura and I got in a heated argument about the Beatles. She said that their morals are atrocious. It wasn't a very friendly argument, and now she probably doesn't like me.

APRIL 10—

I just got through talking to Connie Sothmann. I had to convince her that the Beatles aren't losing popularity. I can see her point, though. I mean, you used to be able to go downtown, and EVERYTHING was Beatles. But not anymore.

They're coming back to the States in August, though, and then it will be just like old times, right?

APRIL 22—

We got a new color T.V. today. We're really lucky. I only have one other friend who has one. Now we can watch the "Sunday Night Movie" in color.

MAY 13—

We went to the "Go-Go" last night. The combo was really "tuff." Got a L-O-N-G letter from my pen pal. She used the word "Beatles" 65 times.

MAY 25—

Went to see "A Hard Day's Night" again yesterday. Funny? I thought I'd die. I had forgotten how hilarious the press conference is.

> *Question: "What do you call that haircut?"*
> *Answer: "Arthur."*

One of my pen pals has seen the movie 12 times. This was my fourth. I wish I could watch the soccer field scene again.

71

I've got to go now to watch "Man from U.N.C.L.E." I love Illya. He's no Rock Hudson, but he's British, you know.

MAY 27—
Mom and Dad are really pressuring me about the Beatles again. For one thing, I'm going to redecorate my room, but Mom says she will not spend any money on it unless I take down my Beatle pictures. She says it's "high time I get over this nonsense."

Also, they won't let me use any more of their stamps or envelopes for anything having to do with the Beatles. They found out I've been sending my British pen pal her letters by airmail, at 15 cents an ounce. Once it cost me $1.75 to send a letter.

JUNE 2—
I got my issue of "Beatles Monthly" today. There was a note attached saying that this is the last issue of my subscription.

Only two more days of school!

CHAPTER 8

"Yesterday"

JUNE 10—

Well, she finally did it. Mom cracked the whip and made me take it all down today. All my Beatle stuff came off the walls. What a sad, sad thing. I wrote this poem to honor the occasion.

> *"Your Beatle pictures must finally come down,"*
> *Said my mum today with an angry frown.*
> *"Oh, no!" I wailed. "Please, Dad, be kind.*
> *And make my mother change her mind!"*
> *"I agree with your mother," my dear dad said.*
> *"But Dad!" "No buts!" he shook his head.*
>
> *I went to my room and on the bed sat.*
> *Take down the Beatles? How can I do that?*
> *"Never mind," Ringo's picture seemed to say.*
> *"Tomorrow will be a better day."*
> *"Buck up," said George. "It's not all that bad.*
> *There's no need to look all that sad."*
>
> *To take them all down took all afternoon.*
> *It looked bloody barren in my room.*
> *The pictures were piled on my bed and floor,*

> *And some were falling out of the door.*
> *They were crammed into suitcases which only just shut,*
> *Then into the attic, the Beatles were put.*

JUNE 18—

Happy birthday, Paul McCartney!

I'm losing interest in writing to my pen pals. Sometimes I think they are kind of immature. They don't seem to be interested in anything except the Beatles. One is starting a "Keep the Beatles Alive" Fan Club in Michigan.

I still love the Beatles music, and I never miss the chance to read about them. I'm interested in everything about them, but I'm interested in other things, too.

For instance, Kelly Conger. He is so nice. I really, really like him. We are going to have lots of fun this summer.

JUNE 25—

Get this! My pen pal in Michigan has a pen pal in Florida who has a friend whose father is a barber and while THEY were in Florida on their first tour, he cut George's and Ringo's hair. The girl in Florida sent my pen pal in Michigan some of their hair and she sent me a piece of George's. I'm enclosing it forever in this diary to see, smell and everything else.

JULY 6—

We got a new air-conditioned Wildcat today. What a car!

Kelly and I are having a great summer. We've got a neat medley of folk songs worked up on the guitar.

JULY 7—
Sue came over today and we talked. It was Ringo's birthday, but I guess we've grown out of celebrating Beatle birthdays.

JULY 20—
John's son, John Charles Julian Lennon, Jr., was in the paper today. He is called Julian for short. He's got a "lovely, adorable, wee face," as they would say in England. I wonder if he will be a singer like his dad?

JULY 29—
I watched "Where the Action Is" with a couple of friends today. Sonny and Cher were on, singing "Baby Don't Go." I love that song. As a matter of fact, I love all their songs, but they really are dumb-looking, aren't they? I mean, Sonny's beaver (or whatever) jackets are just too weird.

I love Cher's hair and earrings, but I'd never wear those bell-bottomed pants. Some of my friends have made themselves a pair to goof around in at parties.

AUGUST 3—

Brenda wrote today pleading for me not to quit writing to her. She is worried because I have really slacked off. She wants me to pledge that I will write   till death do us part, in sickness (Beatlemania) and in health, until our letters sound like this:

Dear Mary,

Well, my 14th grandchild was born today. His name is George. He was born with a perfect Beatle haircut.

Brother, she's nuts! This is the same girl who still sends hate mail to Patti Boyd.

AUGUST 5—

Connie and I went downtown today. I got "The Beatles Story" album. Sometimes it seems that I have lost interest in the Beatles. Sue and I don't see each other very much, so I just don't talk or think about them as much anymore.

But when I played "The Beatles Story" tonight, I realized that all of this is going to be with me forever. It just takes something to remind me and trigger the memories.

The record begins with screams from a Beatle concert. THAT feeling I will never forget.

Sometimes I wish I could turn back the clock and have it all happen again. It was all so marvelous . . . so great . . . so incredible. I wish things could be that way again.

AUGUST 9—

Tom Jones was on T.V. last night. He was unbelievably vulgar. I just sat there with my mouth open. How do they let that stuff on T.V.?

Only eight more days and the Beatles will be in America.

AUGUST 16—

I wish they would play "Help!" on the radio. I've only heard it once. John has a new book out. I'd give anything to have it.

AUGUST 19—

I am so glad we have color T.V. This fall I'll get to see "Hullabaloo" in color. I like "Hullabaloo" better than "Shindig."

My pen pal in England sent me some English money today. She also accused me of losing interest in the Beatles. I haven't! I will love the Beatles until I die!

AUGUST 22—

I am really burned up at the grownups who say that our music and songs aren't "fit to hear." There's nothing wrong with them unless you have an evil mind!

AUGUST 24—

Tomorrow is the day I've been dreading all summer—registration day. I don't know how I'm ever going to get back into the routine. Kelly and I have had so much fun this summer. I wish it were only starting instead of ending.

AUGUST 27—

Ever since the Beatles came over here on tour the papers have been filled with clippings. I can't wait to read the newspaper each night.

My poor pen pal in Virginia. At the last minute her parents wouldn't let her go to Georgia to see the Beatles, even though she had saved all summer for her trip. They said there were too many race riots going on in Georgia. Maybe someday we'll be able to understand what makes parents do the things they do.

I read a few days ago that the Beatles don't believe in "the colour bar." (I certainly don't, either!) They said they have too much respect for Negro musicians.

AUGUST 31—

We finally got in to see "Help!" The first day we went, we were 1 hour, 30 minutes early, but the line was already down the block and around the corner. Everyone was pushing, so we left.

The whole show was so funny. But there were no screams at this one. People just laughed instead. It was an entirely different kind of movie from "A Hard Day's Night."

"Help" has been the No. 1 record the past few weeks. It only took a couple of weeks for it to reach the top of the heap. Of course, that's no surprise. It was destined for the top, as is every Beatle record.

SEPTEMBER 1—

School started today, and I already have homework up to my ears. I didn't have a thing to wear today, so I went downtown tonight and charged four new outfits. Mom and Dad hit the ceiling.

The Beatles are going to be on "Ed Sullivan" September 12 and sing six songs. It's been almost a year since I saw them in Chicago. I can't wait!

SEPTEMBER 2—

"Yesterday" is the new Beatles song. It is BEATLE-FUL! Paul sings it alone. It was the number one top requested song on WLS tonight. This was the first time I've heard it. I don't know if it's from their album or not.

SEPTEMBER 3—

There was an article in the paper today saying that the Beatles aren't as popular anymore because people don't scream at "Help!" Maybe it's because we want to watch and catch every little thing instead of screaming! Did they ever think of that?

SEPTEMBER 10—

I sent my pen pal some of the Beatle cards she said she wanted. I have triplicates of so many that I could spare them. But no way would I ever part with No. 42!

Sue called me today. Shock! I wish we could be best friends again.

SEPTEMBER 13—

I watched the Beatles on Ed Sullivan tonight. I expected to get that same old feeling, but I didn't. I didn't scream or cry or get goose bumps or anything. So what's wrong with me?

I still love them dearly, and I couldn't live without their music, but it's just not the same. I don't feel like I have to go out and buy everything with the word Beatles on it anymore, either.

I remember all the fun I've had because of the Beatles, and I know that none of that can ever happen again.

SEPTEMBER 15—

"Yesterday" has made music history. It's the first song ever to make No. 1 its first week on the survey. Is that great, or is that great?

SEPTEMBER 16—

Ringo and Maureen named their baby Zack. Are they serious? ZACK!?

We play Assumption tomorrow in the first game of the season. I've got $5 on the game.

SEPTEMBER 22—

Rolling Stones were on Red Skelton last night. They sang "Carol," "Tell Me," and "It's All Over Now."

SEPTEMBER 28—

I just got through eating supper. Dad always watches the news while we eat, so we sit there night after night and watch soldiers die. Not very appetizing.

OCTOBER 3—

Boy! You should have heard what my American History teacher said today about the Beatles. It was HORRID! I wonder if it could possibly be true. He said that he heard it on a radio program called "Life Line." According to him, this program claimed that the Beatles openly admitted to being athiests. Their press manager doesn't believe in God, either, and he says that even to him, their morals are atrocious.

A girl in my class said that they are creeps, anyway. I made her wish she hadn't said that.

OCTOBER 6—

I've been giving a lot of thought to my career lately. I want to be a psychiatrist or psychologist when I get out of school.

Then I can figure out why girls are so berserk over the Beatles.

Or, I'd like to be a photographer, or a newspaper reporter. I'd love to spend my life interviewing famous and interesting people.

OCTOBER 10—

We're getting ready for Homecoming this week. No time to write.

NOVEMBER 20—

Geometry, geometry, geometry!

NOVEMBER 28—

I miss you, Dear Diary.

My family today—from left to right—Courtney, Mary Mack Conger, Kelly, and Olivia.
My husband Kelly is the same Kelly mentioned in the diary!

"P.S. I Love You"

JANUARY 13, 1989—

And so I outgrew the Disneyland of those early Beatle years.

But as I grew older, so did the Beatles. They dropped their kiddie image and wrote new songs for the sixties, about love and peace and living free. Their popularity never waned.

Now, it's been nearly a quarter of a century since I began writing in this diary. John F. Kennedy would be 71 years old. George Harrison is an aging baby-boomer rock star, Ringo is a miniature train conductor on a TV series for kids, Paul is a millionaire, and John is dead.

Me? I'm still living and writing in Iowa, still dreaming of seeing the queen and castles of England someday.

Waxing nostalgic, I sent some letters off to my old pen pals, whose letters I have saved among my Beatle memorabilia for over two decades.

Brenda Conner Tuten of Roanoke, Virginia, writes: "We were really crazy, weren't we? I would have hated to miss that part of my life. I felt excited, in love, crazy and silly. Most of all happy. I needed that."

And from Sally Whittock Schofield in England: "Regarding those lovely Beatles, I still obtain much pleasure from the memories of those times. I feel the Beatles helped me to grow up. We felt we could go wild, a little—but for me, anyway, it was a sort of innocence."

Me, too.

The memories of those early Beatle years will stay with me for all my days. Especially, I'll never forget a teenaged girl in Chicago on September 5, 1964. She's still waving her red Beatle banner, and reliving her "Sweet Beatle Dreams."